MW00511718

Get REAL
A Practical Guide to Leading Adolescent Groups

Get REAL
A Practical Guide to Leading Adolescent Groups

Beth Harris Brandes and Judy B. Ingold

Families International, Inc., Milwaukee, Wisconsin 53224

Illustrations by James Macleod

Copyright 1997 Families International, Inc.
11700 West Lake Park Drive
Milwaukee, WI 53224

Publishing in association with Family Service America, Inc.

All rights reserved. No part of this book may be repro-
duced, stored in a retrieval system, or transmitted in any
form or by any means (electronic, mechanical, photocopy-
ing, recording, or otherwise) without permission in writing
from the publisher.

To our husbands, Rand and Charles,
and our sons, Blake and Daniel

CONTENTS

ACKNOWLEDGMENTS

Thanks to . . .

- Pat Hensley, Fran Kaplan, Dr. Michael Carrera, Dr. Stephen Bavolek, and Linda Riggsbee for reviewing this manuscript and offering helpful suggestions
- TEEN UP program staff, who show creativity, compassion, and professionalism daily in their group work with adolescents
- Bobby K. Boyd, Andrea Benfield, the board and staff of Catawba County Social Services, Libby Sigmon, and the three school systems in our county for believing in prevention services
- Chaplain William Hall, Judy's mentor, friend, and teacher of group facilitation for 20 years
- Florence Flanders, Beth's seventh-grade English teacher, who made her write
- Barbara Huberman, who first told us about Families International
- The hundreds of teens who have trusted us and one another in groups
- Our parents, grandparents, children, and husbands for teaching us to love, laugh, and learn

INTRODUCTION

Using REAL Skills With Teenagers

Leading groups with teens is a lot like learning to drive a car. A little driver's education helps. But because the road conditions are constantly changing, you need to stay alert, flexible, and committed to the journey. The first time you drive in snow, it's a little scary. But once you learn how to handle a skid on ice, you will gain confidence. As group leaders, we are always expanding our repertoire of "driving skills"—learning from others and the teens themselves. Experience helps us all relax.

Because no two teens or groups are ever the same, our best advice to new group leaders is to "be REAL."

R: Reflect what teens say and what they communicate nonverbally.

E: Explore what's going on. Don't assume you know their feelings.

A: Attend to the emotions behind the words and behaviors.

L: Loan teens tools to help them solve problems.

Being REAL means learning to listen. Teens will forgive many blunders if they know the leaders respect and care for them. And they usually learn best from people they trust.

Being REAL also means recognizing that teens are not adults. Groups with teens require a different awareness and set of skills on the part of the group leader. Keep in mind that adolescence is a time of big feet, big ideas, and big appetites. Early adolescence is a time of rapid physical growth, so teens need space to sprawl out and a group room they can move around in. Teen groups also need a range of activities that provide physical movement and ways to burn off energy. They also love food that begins with P: pizza, potato chips, and pretzels!

Teens' moods may shift rapidly. Try not to take it personally. Instead, reflect and explore troubling verbal and nonverbal behaviors (remember: REAL). Reinforce the healthy behaviors that you see.

Keep in mind that early adolescents are tackling many developmental tasks. Teens are often:

- extremely self-conscious and self-focused
- actively seeking acceptance from their peers
- moving from a concrete way of perceiving the world to more abstract thinking
- experimenting with new identities and developing values, both in and outside the group
- pushing for independence, whether they are prepared for it or not

These developmental issues affect the way teens interact with one another and their group leader. They may also affect the way you recruit, build, and facilitate a group for adolescents. The Adolescent Developmental Issues Chart at the end of this section provides a basic road map to guide your journey toward developing your own teen-group program.

Of course, like adults, adolescents are individuals who have a range of learning styles. Some learn by watching, others by hearing, and many by touching, feeling, and acting out roles and responses. Observe preteens and teens to see what activities they enjoy the most. Often a combination of learning activities yields the best results.

We sometimes compare group work to looking through a kaleidoscope of shifting colors, patterns, and movement. As you focus on teens' developmental needs and personalities, you will discover many surprising patterns and connections. These configurations and colors often change. No two groupings are ever quite the same, but each design is distinctive and beautiful in its own way—and every one contains a little bit of magic.

The reflections and tips in this practical guide are designed to help guidance counselors, teachers, social workers, and other youth workers embarking on the teen-group adventure.

The guide is divided into four chapters, each of which focuses on one issue of adolescent development. Each chapter begins by helping the practitioner "tune in" to the issue in a general way and closes by providing a series of practical facilitation tips for working with the developmental issue addressed.

We hope you will enjoy the journey!

DEVELOPMENTAL ISSUES IN ADOLESCENCE AND IMPLICATIONS FOR GROUPS

Adolescents are . . .

SELF-CONSCIOUS
- Anxious about image of group
- May easily become embarrassed, reticent, silly
- Vulnerable to peers
- Concerned about body image
- Obsessed with mirrors, hair, designer tennis shoes
- Respond to personal recognition

SELF-FOCUSED
- May need structured ways to empathize with others
- Unaware how behavior affects others in group
- May compete for group time
- Fragile emotionally in response to disappointments or tragedies in peer group

SEEKING PEER ACCEPTANCE
- Need emotional safety
- May exaggerate to belong to group
- Group can be impetus for positive change

GAINING INDEPENDENCE
- Slow to trust adults
- Test limits/authority
- Need ownership in group

- Need clear boundaries
- Need incremental freedom and responsibilities

DEVELOPING IDENTITY

- May idealize group leader
- May attempt to "split off" group leaders from each other
- May be zealous about group
- Experimenting with personal styles of dress and behavior
- Developing a repertoire of coping behaviors

EXPERIENCING RAPID GROWTH AND MOOD SWINGS

- Moods may swing high or low in group
- Short attention span
- Need energizers and physical activity

MOVING FROM CONCRETE TO MORE ABSTRACT THINKING

- May describe issues in black and white
- May be judgmental
- Literal in responses
- Need experiential learning
- Need step-by-step direction
- Little use for insight
- Prefer "here and now" demonstrations
- Romanticize future events, feel invulnerable
- Short-term reinforcement

DEVELOPING SENSE OF FUTURE

- Undaunted by "fear tactics"

(continued)

- Limited understanding of consequences
- Need experiences that reinforce consequences
- Limited ability to transfer learning

GAINING SKILLS AND VALUES
- Need skill practice
- Respond well to short-term rewards
- Still open to change
- Impressionable
- Positive peer pressure can make a difference

Adapted from original work by Linda Barr, M.N., and Catherine Monserrat, Ph.D., *Working with Childbearing Adolescents*, 1980, revised 1996, New Futures, Inc., 5400 Cutler NE, Albuquerque, NM 87110.

Self-Consciousness, Self-Focus, Self-Absorption, or ME, ME, ME!

As young teens grow and mature, they are often highly self-conscious. They frequently compare themselves physically to their peers and worry whether they are "normal." Watching themselves in the mirror becomes a daily ritual as they attempt to integrate rapid changes and a new, independent sense of self. They are sensitive to labels and easily embarrassed. Above all, they don't want to look stupid in front of their peers. Many would rather suffer in silence than risk being a part of a group that is not "cool."

Young teens usually respond eagerly to personal attention and individual challenges. Often they either love to talk about themselves or find discussing personal issues very difficult. They are legitimately concerned about confidentiality in groups because they know how other teenagers like to talk. And even though their verbal skills may be well-developed, teens often must learn how to listen to others. Empathizing with another teenager's problems is a learned skill.

Tips for Group Leaders

Make the group a positive symbol and a socially acceptable one.

Even if the group is built around a negative issue such as divorce, death, or academic underachievement, sell it to teens, name it, and label the work of the group in positive terms. Teen group names such as Teen Challenge, TOPS, and Teens in Charge all connote positive action. One middle-school group dealing with loss and death was called "Good Grief." A teen pregnancy prevention group was called TEEN UP. Another group for children of alcoholic parents was called C.H.A.N.G.E.S. (Children Hurt by Alcoholism: Now Growing, Educating, Sharing). Teens can create acronyms for groups, too. Try sponsoring a contest among group members and give an award for the winning group name.

At-risk children may be particularly sensitive to labels that seem to reinforce their problems or insecurities. In dealing with teens with special needs or difficult problems, you may want to think of ways to reframe why teens have been invited to join. A group of teens who were foster children, for example, preferred the name "Learning to Live on My Own" to one that highlighted their status as foster children. In establishing a group for eighth graders who had repeated a grade and were experimenting with risky behaviors, we explained that they had been referred because they had had "life experiences that had made them grow up fast." We added that their teachers thought they were mature enough to handle the topics we planned to discuss. Many of them knew they were considered "at risk," but there was no need to rub it in their faces. This explanation for their being recruited also offered them a new way of reframing their experiences. When one student noted that the group didn't include any "preps," another student commented that perhaps "preps" weren't mature enough to handle the conversation.

At the first group meeting, begin learning names and devise ways for every group member to have a chance to talk.

Use name tags, name games, or whatever it takes—but learn teenagers' names. Also tell them specifically what you want to be called. We have always felt comfortable with teenagers calling us by our first names, even when we were leading school groups in places where teachers were addressed by their last names, but you should use what you find comfortable.

Ensuring opportunities for each member to talk early in the process helps alleviate anxiety and promotes a sense of personal belonging to the group. Especially during the first few sessions of the group, leaders may want to use a brief structured activity as a get-acquainted exercise or springboard for discussion. If written, the

activity should be very simple to ensure that poor readers can participate fully. All members of the group need
a chance to express themselves, however briefly, because
it lowers their anxiety and it establishes each member
equally as part of the group.

See the end of this chapter for a Sampler of Get-
Acquainted Activities, Icebreakers, and Rounds.[1]

> *Teens respond favorably to individual attention, pro-
> jects that belong to them, and personal challenges
> in group.*

Like all of us, young teens especially love personal
attention and recognition of their unique identity. Self-
decorated notebooks, name tags, photos, and records of
accomplishments all rank high on the list. Leaders may
want to make a group chart or bulletin board with all
members' names and pictures, on which teens can chart
goals, group attendance, school attendance, and so
forth. Certificates and other forms of recognition for
group participation can also be very significant for teens
who are unaccustomed to receiving public approval for
their accomplishments.

Children who have very few belongings or little personal space at home like projects that they can keep
and show off. Decorated keepsake boxes, scrapbooks,
or craft projects are often particularly important to
these children.

Door prizes or incentives for group attendance should
also have personal utility and genuine appeal. Picture

---

1. Contributors to this list of activities include Sandy Robbins, Duuna Gill,
Kathy Young-Shugar, Vivian Coleman, Tracey Paul, Tamara Dempsey-Tan-
ner, and Mary Linkous.

frames, school supplies, jewelry, and vouchers for burgers or CDs are often popular among young teens. If working with teen moms, you may find they like personal gifts more than they appreciate gifts for their babies. You should be aware, however, that what may seem useful to you may seem very uncool to a teenager. We once had to beg teens to take a contribution of socks and gloves off our hands.

Using incentives for groups should be carefully considered. We have found that the promise of food or a small gift does attract teens to a group event initially, and for some teens a concrete reward can be a reinforcement at each meeting. Many teen pregnancy prevention programs offer low-income teens a dollar a day for attending group and avoiding pregnancy. Some programs also offer a cumulative reward for group participants (for instance, a pizza party or amusement park outing) or special recognition for participants who meet certain attendance requirements in group. But, in our experience, a concrete incentive alone does not sustain a teen's attendance or participation in a group activity. Teens often tell us that they attended groups because they felt loved, cared for, respected, and listened to in the group setting. They also like the fun and sense of belonging that can flow from a group that is working together. Concrete incentives may be an extra attraction, but teens also need to believe that the group will value them as people, that they will not be judged or stereotyped unfairly, and that they will have a chance to succeed and to belong.

Establish a five-minute check-in at the beginning of group.

Use this time to attend to the immediate needs or collective mood of the teens. A five-minute check-in at the beginning of each meeting often gives group members time to bring up burning issues that may affect their learning or participation during the rest of the group time.

For instance, it is helpful to know if Julie just had a falling out with her boyfriend in the hall or if Steven is upset by some event at home. With young teens, the leader may need to ask for input specifically. "Since last week, has anything especially exciting, good, upsetting, or frustrating happened?" Be prepared to hear anything, from the most benign event to the most devastating. The challenge is to listen.

You can also pick up clues to members' moods from individual or group nonverbal behavior: "Susan, you look really sad today" or "This group is really wound up this morning. What's happening?" Another quick way to assess moods is to go around and ask each teen in the circle, "What color describes you today? What does the color mean to you?" Leaders can draw on information from these check-in activities throughout the life of the group.

Occasionally, a question may uncover a deeper issue, so leaders need to explore between the lines of an answer. Sometimes, you can almost instinctively guess the bigger issue, but be careful not to assume. Begin by reflecting the answer ("Sounds like you feel . . ." "Sounds like you've been thinking a lot about . . ."). Then explore the statement, using phrases such as "how," "in what way," "tell me a little more," to understand what the teen is really saying.

If a group member discloses information during the check-in that needs the group's or leader's response, the leader may need to forgo a structured activity and explore the issue presented by the teen. For example, during a check-in period the group leader learned that a teen's grandmother had died. The leader chose to focus on the loss before moving ahead with the planned activity. The leader inquired about the teen's experience and then asked other teens in the group if they had ever lost a grandparent or someone they cared for deeply. Offering support and understanding in such circumstances is more important than staying with the curriculum.

If the group seems restless or distracted by the attention given to one member, the leader might comment that "Susan is really upset right now and needs a chance to talk about how she feels, but I know some of you want to continue with our planned activity today. Should we talk about this for five more minutes and then continue?" or "Susan, would you feel OK talking with me individually about this after group?" The challenge is to balance the needs of the individual and the group as well as to help teens learn ways to express their own needs.

During the first few group sessions, watch for nonverbal cues, especially from reticent members of the group. Young adolescents often seek attention and ask for help in indirect ways.

Remember, don't assume that you know what is going on. Check it out. Often, introverted members of a group appear uninterested or depressed when they are merely timid. On the other hand, if a student displays a pattern of depressive behaviors, you need to attend to his or her needs. Use the REAL formula to explore the emotions behind the behaviors and find out whether a significant problem exists.

Minor self-destructive behaviors are often a teen's primary way of getting attention. Pierced noses and ears with twelve rings has never been our favorite look, but many teens adopt nihilistic looks, dress, and behavior to signal their independence. Before you try to extinguish a behavior, you probably need to give the teen a replacement behavior — another way he or she can gain attention from you and the group or another role that offers a different identification. In this case, the leader might ignore the negative attention-getting devices (i.e., drawing tattoos on one's arms, multi-pierced ear lobes) or reflect: "Looks like you can stand a lot of pain. How did you learn to do that?" The leader also can try to reinforce positive behaviors honestly: "You know, Susan, I'm not really into multiple earrings, but you have a great flair for picking out artistic ones. How about helping me with the design of the poster for the group?"

On other occasions, you may need to consider nonverbal behaviors occurring outside the group setting. For example, in one group, a teen frequently rolled her sleeve up, revealing a bandage on her arm. When the leader inquired about the injury, the teen refused to comment. However, after group, the leader followed up with the student and discovered that the teen was cutting herself with a razor blade. Obviously, the group leader needed to pay attention to this self-destructive behavior, even though it represented a negative way of getting attention. Chapter 3, on concrete thinking, contains other suggestions on exploring nonverbal behaviors.

In groups, indicate clear beginnings and endings of events.

Structure helps alleviate members' anxiety about what the group will be doing. Present clear agendas, time frames, and structure for group activities and meetings. It's helpful at the first meeting to distribute a handout listing meeting dates and topics to be covered.

Give specific feedback to teens about their behaviors.

In No More Nagging, Nitpicking and Nudging,[2] Jim Wiltens suggests a model for giving immediate feedback to teens.

• **Catch them.** Catch teens when they are behaving positively and constructively. Immediate feedback is more helpful to teens than general statements about their attitudes or characteristics. Positive reinforcement encourages positive behavior and ensures that teens behaving disruptively do not get more attention than those who try to succeed.

• **Praise them.** Identify the positive behavior in specific terms: "I appreciate the way you organized your materials for class." "I noticed you were angry at Bob, but you expressed yourself without yelling or hurting his feelings."

---

2. Jim Wiltens, *No More Nagging, Nitpicking, and Nudging* (Sunnyvale, CA: Deer Crossing Press, 1991).

• **Use "I" messages.** Start sentences with "I" to show how the undesirable behaviors affect you. "You" sentences often sound blaming and create defensiveness on the part of the teen.

• **Reinforce.** Teens often say adults nag too much. Try reinforcing positive behaviors with written signs or one-word reminders (i.e., "Quiet Zone" or "Leadership"). Use a hand signal to quiet a group. Label storage boxes with signs—Pencils, Sign-in Sheets, Recycle Cans—to remind teens to take care of their own materials.

• **Ask teens to "recall" for clarification.** Ask the teen to tell you what they understood you to say. This technique helps clarify what the teens heard. As teens actually say (or write down) the positives they hear, they physically reinforce the concept in their minds. This repetition is the first step to incorporating a new behavior.

> *Facilitate the discussion so that each member has a chance to be heard.*

After young teens discover that they have a listening audience, they often can talk nonstop—seemingly without breathing!—with little regard for others in the group. They are not necessarily being selfish; they are just so involved in their own personal issues that they may have little awareness of how their behavior affects the group. Sometimes their stories can also be convoluted and tangential, which may result in other group members losing interest. The leader should acknowledge the earnest talker's feelings ("Jeremy, you've got so much on your mind") but then may need to ask the teen to focus ("We're running short on time" or "We have about three more minutes to discuss this"). Another tactic is to ask for a summary point: "Could you tell the group the most important/difficult/frustrating thing that happened?" Depending on the ego strength of the teen talking, the leader may also ask the group if members want the teen to continue, although leaders should note how difficult it is for teens to confront one another gently. They will often either avoid the confrontation or be mercilessly blunt. You may opt to give the feedback yourself, especially if you feel peer feedback may make the teen feel defensive or hurt.

• **Redirect the conversation.** Cutting short a group member's monologue or redirecting an adolescent group member is sometimes necessary to balance the needs of the individual and the group. The leader's tone and style can convey positive regard while still moving ahead. Keep the group discussion focused and encourage participation by all. You may have to elicit responses from quiet members or redirect dominant ones more actively than you would in an adult group.

Sometimes teens don't listen to one another very carefully; they may interrupt or change the topic entirely in group right after another group member has spilled his or her guts. The group leader may need to intervene at this point to ask a teen to "hold that thought" until the other teen has finished making his or her point.

At times, one group member's disclosure may prompt a therapeutic watershed, when several teens reveal secrets or admit similar experiences.

These disclosures may offer an opportunity for the group to grow and bond together. However, leaders should be aware of how upsetting and difficult it is to listen to emotionally charged stories. Watch for nonverbal clues (tears, fidgeting, and so forth) that signal limits to the group's attention span or a particular member's need for support.

Young teens may also compete to tell the most dramatic story in group as a way of gaining attention, acceptance, or status. This can lead to contagious outbreaks of dramatic and exaggerated disclosures. If you sense that children are beginning to fabricate stories, attempt to make a summary statement, noting the key needs that have been expressed.

AND THEN, THE LITTLE GREEN ALIEN SAID TO ME...

Certainly there is a danger of overfacilitating or overcontrolling a teen group and interfering with the power of the group process, but a leader's skillful interventions can also help teens gain focus and utilize group time effectively.

A SAMPLER OF GET-ACQUAINTED ACTIVITIES, ICEBREAKERS, AND ROUNDS

BINGO

Design your own grid with each square containing one personal characteristic, such as "good sense of humor." Pass out copies of the bingo grid and let each person circle all the characteristics that apply to him or her. Ask "Who has Bingo?" and have these players read their bingo line to the group. This is a good, nonthreatening way to introduce group members and help them note what they have in common.

NAME GAMES

Tell the group your name and a characteristic that begins with the first letter of your first name (e.g., "Friendly Fran"). Tell us your name and an animal that you think is a lot like you—or an animal that you like.

BEAN BAG OR YARN TOSS

Throw a bean bag around the group. When a person catches it, he or she should describe a personal strength, something he or she is good at, or another characteristic of your choosing. With the yarn toss, members stand or sit in a circle. The leader takes a ball of yarn, holds the end of the yarn and tosses the ball to another member across the circle. The person who catches the yarn says

(continued)

one thing he or she has learned or what she or he feels about some event. As each member holds a section of the yarn, the group creates a web. Note how the group of individuals is now connected. This web can then be tacked on a bulletin board or floor to symbolize group connectedness.

FOUR CORNERS

Cut pictures from magazines to illustrate the following categories: my favorite food, something I like to do, something I want to improve, and something I like about me. Ask participants to paste the four pictures or words on construction paper. Use this "poster" to introduce yourself to the group.

TOILET PAPER TOSS

Pass a roll of toilet paper around the group. Ask each person to take as many sheets as he or she wants. After the roll has gone around, ask group members to tell one thing about themselves for each sheet they have.

GET-ACQUAINTED SCAVENGER HUNT

Have members move around the group with a sheet of paper to get autographs of people who fit various descriptions, for example, someone who works with adolescent groups, someone who sings with a musical group, someone who is the oldest in his or her family. (This icebreaker can be adapted for large conference groups as well as smaller support groups.)

"FEELINGS" CHECK-IN ROUNDS

● On a scale of 1 to 10, how are you feeling right now about _____ ?
● Tell me in one word how you feel about your family/this group _____

JELLY BEAN ICEBREAKER

Prepare a bowl of loose M & Ms, jelly beans, or some other colored candies. Make up a color chart as follows:

● Yellow – Tell us your favorite color.
● Red – Tell us who is your hero/heroine.
● Green – Tell us something you like to do.
● Blue – Tell us something you are afraid of.

(You can also substitute review topics or different self-disclosure requests on the chart.)

Ask all participants to choose one or more colored candies. Then show them the color chart and ask them to respond to the instruction corresponding to the color of the candies they picked. Each person gets to eat his or her candy after responding.

MAGIC STICK ACTIVITY

Prepare an ordinary stick or wand that group members can name, paint, or decorate as they like to make it a "magic stick." Tell participants that this is their chance to be actors. Each person must take the magic stick and "turn it into something" in front of the others. For example, the magic stick could be a golf club, steering wheel, curling iron, twirling baton, antenna, and so forth. As each

(continued)

member acts out a scene with the magic stick, the other participants must guess what they are demonstrating.

Reinforce the members' great acting achievement by putting colorful, adhesive stars on their faces or hands. Remind them that "The real magic is inside of you!"

CHAPTER 2

The Need to Belong and Be Accepted by Peers

A teen's self-consciousness and need for peer approval affect his or her initial decision to join a group. These factors also affect the interaction within a group dramatically.

Positive Peers

Teens can be powerful influences on one another, positively and negatively. Group members can promote healthy new ways of communicating and coping with problems. If a respected group member expresses sadness or acknowledges that he or she is not always confident, other teens may feel it is OK to express their honest emotions too. The endorsement of an activity by a

popular member can encourage other teens to try something new or stretch themselves. Collectively, members
shore each other up to sustain a group norm that may
be unpopular or uncool outside the group.

Teens can also redefine what is "smart," such as
staying in school or not being a parent until the teen is
financially capable of supporting a child. Groups of
low-income teens who themselves had been targeted as
the recipients of charitable community services shifted
that identity through a series of volunteer projects in
their neighborhood. They became volunteers who
helped others, reframing their image personally and collectively. In these activities, young adolescents offered
each other new ideas and strategies to deal with negative peer pressure.

Group Selection

Whenever it is possible to do so, try to interview
teens individually before grouping them with others.
This one-on-one interview helps you glimpse how the
teen processes information and perceives the value or
threat of a group experience. Ask the teen to tell you
about a group he or she belongs to and note what is
good, difficult, or memorable about that group experience. During this exchange, you can also determine
whether the teen has special needs or fears concerning
group involvement.

In forming a group, leaders may strive to recruit
members who have similar needs but should also delib-
erately try to select teens who offer different strengths
to one another. The facilitator should look for heteroge-
neous styles: balancing talkers with quiet kids, leaders

and followers, and so forth. Group facilitators should also consider skill levels and behavioral issues. For example, a group composed entirely of behaviorally and emotionally handicapped eighth-grade boys could send a counselor to an early grave if he or she plans to conduct a "talk-focused group." Together such boys need intense structure. Yet, one or two boys who are diagnosed with attention-deficit hyperactivity disorder might benefit from being in a group with less active boys who won't reinforce distractible or disruptive behavior.

Preteens may need more structure and physical activity than an older group does. They may need more concrete activities to begin discussions. Sometimes younger teens get very silly and giggly unless tasks are clearly assigned. They may not have the capacity to concentrate for long periods of time if they are not physically tackling a project. At the same time, some preteens act more maturely than do 15-year-olds. In our experience, certain age groupings (12- to 14-year-olds together and 15- to 18-year-olds together) generally work in terms of activity level, because they are consistent with middle school and high school age divisions. However, teens of any age respond best to experiential learning, rather than "talk-only" approaches.

Physical and emotional maturity levels can also vary widely among teens of the same age. Teenage boys often physically mature later than girls do, but they are nonetheless sorting out similar issues (pubertal changes, the presence or absence of romantic feelings, concerns about mortality). We try to address what we see and create a context of acceptance, so teens will know that they all carry their own clock inside them.

Don't make assumptions about maturity on the basis of physical appearances. If a 12-year-old girl looks 18, she probably is eliciting responses from the opposite sex that she may not fully understand. She may still think like a 12-year-old. Likewise, a 13-year-old can appear very logical and focused one minute and forget his lunch money the next.

Because the adolescent years are a time of great change and growth, both physically and psychologically, it is best not to lump all teens from 12 to 18 years of age together in a group. The range in age, interests, and maturity is simply too great. Instead, build groups with age and maturity in mind: preteens (11 to 12 years old) grouped together, early adolescents (13 to 14 years old) together, and so forth.

Considerable debate surrounds the issue of whether adolescents benefit more from single-sex or coed groups. Certainly both kinds of groups have benefits, limitations, and special considerations. However, we prefer single-sex groups for discussing sexuality issues with young adolescents because, in general, 12- to 14-year-old boys are less physically and emotionally mature than their female counterparts. Girls at this age tend to be more verbally sophisticated and affiliative in group settings and can often dominate boys verbally in exchanges. Boys are likely to be forced on the defensive and mask many feelings that would be disclosed more readily in a single-sex group.

However, there are benefits to facilitating structured coed discussion—as opposed to therapeutic—groups among 12- to 14-year-olds. Exchanging a slate of questions between a girls' group and a boys' group at this age often promotes very positive dialogue; it helps for both boys and girls to discuss the questions separately beforehand, then come together for a joint discussion.

Coed groups with older teens appear to be quite beneficial and more equitable, but the group may need to deal with the dynamics of romantic alliances and breakups in group, which may disrupt or intensify exchanges between group members.

Building Relationships

In the early stages of groups, leaders may discover that young teens relate primarily to the group leader. The teens will often seek approval or feedback directly from the adult leader instead of looking to peers for response. Gradually, as the leader facilitates new alliances among group members, the teens will seek out peer opinions and depend less on the adult leader.

Group leaders should constantly look for ways to build bridges between members and to break up or rearrange cliques, whether they be single-sex or coed groupings. Leaders should tune in to group scapegoating, intimidating behaviors, and children who lie to get acceptance from the group.

Tips for Group Leaders

In structured group activities, rearrange seating or pair up unlikely partners.

A few techniques for rearranging the group are:
- Match partners by color of eyes or pieces of a puzzle.

• Call "switch seats" spontaneously or play musical chairs with popular music.

• Tape matching phrases, numbers, and so forth under different chairs so unlikely partners will have to meet.

• Have teens sign their names on a numbered list when they enter the room. Then match numbers 2 and 4, 1 and 3, and so on.

See the list of Activities in Dyads at the end of this chapter for more techniques for getting group members to interact in different constellations.

> *During group discussions, point out similarities among group members' experiences.*

Note such links as when group members have tackled a difficult problem, moved to a new place, or resolved a similar issue. However, be careful not to assume that the same sort of event always evokes the same feelings in teens. Teens can be at different places in a continuum of feelings and can sometimes minimize another's initial reaction to an event. For example, one girl may be devastated by news of her pregnancy, but another may be thrilled; a child who has resolved a loss experience may have little recall of her initial response to a loss. Teens, like adults, should avoid saying, "I know just how you feel," but can be taught to be empathic listeners.

> *Structure ways to control the very common practice among seventh and eighth graders of insulting and mercilessly teasing one another. Label "building" versus "breaking" comments to remind younger teens of the implications of their comments.*

A group of seventh- and eighth-grade girls in an after-school program were notorious for trashing one another verbally. The group agreed that if someone "cut" or insulted a person, the girl had to say two good things about the other person—and, interestingly, the group monitored this entirely by themselves. Young teens like structured ways to respond to behaviors; they sometimes will drive a practice into the ground with repetition but at least they get the point.

Assign rotating roles to group members at the beginning of group.

Assigned roles often promote different structured ways of interacting without risking embarrassment or ridicule from peers. Group members can choose the roles from written cards in a basket. Roles might include:
- A Hostess or Host (who gives out refreshments)
- An Encourager (who looks for positive behaviors in each group member and points out those behaviors at the end of the group)
- A Bouncer (who identifies disruptive behaviors and helps the group stay on task)
- A Summarizer (who reports key issues at the end of group)

"BOUNCER"   "ENCOURAGER"

- A Secretary (who calls all absent members or reminds members of certain responsibilities)

Give teens practice in dealing with stereotypes.

Early adolescents are notorious for labeling one another, designating, say, the "geek," the "prep," the "virgin," the "fag," the "stud." They will often enter group with many preconceived notions about other members. Discussions about stereotypes with this age group never seem to have much impact, perhaps because the topic is being discussed abstractly.

Try a game in which group members are given a label randomly. Assign every person a neon color and then arbitrarily decide that the green people don't get refreshments. Or randomly hand out envelopes containing different amounts of play money, and let group members go shopping for a seat in the room, a pencil and paper, their own shoes, snacks, gifts, and so forth. Members can negotiate or barter with other group members. Then let them discuss how it feels to have few resources through no fault of their own, who has power, who shares, and who flaunts their wealth. Watch the learning take place before your eyes.

> *Create safe ways for young teens to ask potentially embarrassing questions or to discuss extremely personal issues.*

One never wants to look dumb in front of his or her peers, but self-consciousness takes on new proportions during early adolescence. In order to protect fragile teen egos, group leaders may want to anticipate certain questions from teens. A group leader can say, "You probably already know this, but a lot of eighth graders (or whoever) ask me . . . ," then answer the question.

Try using a human-interest approach by describing another teen's experience (regarding grief, depression, trying to break up with her abusive boyfriend, and so forth). Stories about other teens fascinate young people, and they often pay closer attention if you use an invented teen example. However, be careful not to use names— and be advised that eighth graders are almost always certain that they know the person you are talking about.

The anonymous question box is a tool that has long been used by counselors, teachers, and other youth workers. Sometimes an edited written list of the questions deposited in the box can be reassuring to young teens, too. They realize they are not the only ones who don't know everything. You may want to collect such lists at the end of the group, especially if they contain sexual content or other sensitive material. These written lists have a tendency to be misrepresented outside the group setting and could jeopardize your group.

Many eighth and ninth grade boys are very homophobic; they shirk from anything that would make them look less than macho. In our experience, young adolescent boys greatly underreport sexual and physical abuse because of this fear. Interestingly, one way to get boys to talk about abuse is by first asking about what girls might feel if they were abused or by asking about how a guy might feel if his sister or mother were abused. Then discuss how a boy might feel if he were abused. Dealing with this issue indirectly at first often allows boys the freedom to acknowledge feelings at a level once removed. Sometimes it also leads to later private disclosure with the group leader.

Sometimes, a teen will bring a best friend to group for support. Acknowledge the group member's enthusiasm in sharing the group with a friend, but assess the pros and cons of a friend's participation in a closed therapeutic group.

At times, an adolescent will eagerly and enthusiastically bring a new member to an already established group. Generally, the leader has not screened this person and does not have parental consent for the teen to participate. The leader should acknowledge the friend and explore the reasons the group member brought him or her. ("Jonah, I see you brought Sandy to group today. What did you want Sandy to know about our group?") If the group is a closed group without open enrollment, the leader may ask the group members how they feel about having an unfamiliar person participate.

Generally, we do not recommend visitors, teen or adult, at closed groups. A visitor will always affect the group process. Whenever it is possible to do so, advise teens of upcoming visitors, such as student interns or other professional staff. We often give the teens themselves a chance to tell the visitor our group rules, key issues of our group, and so on, giving them ownership of the group.

Telling secrets makes teens vulnerable to their peers. Reinforce the principle of confidentiality in group.

Like anyone with a secret, teens worry about what others will think of them or what might happen if they disclose troubling personal information. Teens greatly fear rejection or cruel reprisals—and, unfortunately, this fear is sometimes well founded. In classroom situations, give teens the opportunity for a private audience regarding issues of abuse, gender identity, or any other sensitive topic. If disclosures occur, reiterate the confidentiality rule. Frequently, perhaps every meeting, ask every member to reaffirm verbally his or her commitment to confidentiality regarding specific disclosures. Refer to the list of Group Rules at the end of Chapter 3, which can be posted during meetings to remind members of their responsibility to keep group discussions private.

> *If teens lie to gain acceptance—and you know it—try to deal with them individually about the lie and then attempt to facilitate some resolution in the group.*

Preteens and teens often exaggerate or misrepresent their exploits to gain attention. Interestingly, one lie often turns into many lies in a group, because the group feeds on the story like readers of tabloid newspapers. A leader's observation that "this sounds a little unbelievable" may curb the flow. However, some children need to be confronted individually about this pattern. Generally, if a teen lies, the leader should confront him or her after the group and tell the person that lies break down trust. Give the teen another chance, but remind him or her of the consequences of another lie. With such teens, we mutually agree that next time we will have to have proof of an outrageous assertion from an outside source and follow up with a teacher or parent, if it is necessary to do so.

Lies in group can have even greater consequences. In one group, a girl fabricated an elaborate adoption story that became more incredible as she added details. First, she claimed she was adopted, which came as a great surprise to all of us. By the end of the story, she had met her beautiful, rich biological mother at the local drugstore and discovered that she, the eighth grader, was one of triplets who were also very attractive. After the group, we asked her to stay to talk and told her we thought she had made up the story. She initially denied this adamantly, but as we talked about her great desire to gain attention from the group, she admitted that she had created the entire scenario. We agreed that she needed to tell the group that she had lied to them before the story was spread through the school. When we reconvened the group, one leader sat next to her and introduced her as being very brave and committed to the group. The girl then told the group she had lied, and we discussed what this meant to her and how it affected the group's level of trust in her.

> *Head off group members who try to intimidate the group or the leader with disruptive behavior. Curb those who initiate ritualistic disclosures or suggest potentially harmful ways of belonging to the group.*

We call this the "slumber party syndrome." A group member suddenly suggests that "everybody tell whether you are a virgin" or "tell the grossest thing you ever did to somebody." Generally, this sort of process needs to be halted because it puts children in a no-win situation. Leaders may or may not want to claim it as a teachable moment. To depersonalize the issue, the leader could ask, "Why might someone not want to answer that question?" or "Has anyone ever told something that was a lie just so you would seem like everyone else?" Group leaders may also decide to pull rank and say that this behavior is not appropriate. But sometimes helping teens understand why the behavior is not appropriate is helpful.

Young teens, especially adolescent boys, will often use behaviors such as glaring, acting bored, walking around the room, slouching in chairs, and even sleeping to provoke a group leader's response. Bad language or crude behavior are other ways to unsettle adults and test the limits in a group. Often, a group rule about avoiding slang or foul language will limit this behavior. If it persists, leaders should attempt to defuse the power of such behavior. For example, in a group of high-risk eighth-grade boys, two competed vociferously during the first group session to see who could use the "F" word most often. The leader acted nonchalant, but noted that the "F" word was slang for intercourse and that, in this culture, it had lost most of its meaning as an obscenity. Her rule was that if a member used slang to describe someone or some event, he had to describe it in two other ways without using slang. After calling the boys to this task several times, they stopped using the term altogether. Adults should be aware that many children really do not know what slang words represent. However, children usually do know that slang gets attention and will continue to use it out of habit or because the words seem to wield power.

Teens like to learn things first from their peers, but peer helpers may need adult guidance and backup.

Teen speakers or teen panels can be effective educators, but they can also be an unknown commodity.

Plan ahead and be prepared to facilitate peer exchanges. Ask panelists to write key points on an index card before the panel begins to help the speakers keep their focus. When it is possible to do so, let them practice with your input.

Many programs have used peer helpers successfully. The Natural Helpers Program[1] lets teens determine their own peer helpers by asking the teens to list three other teenagers in their school to whom they would talk to if they had a problem. The natural helpers are thus selected from every subgroup in the school and are trained together in an intensive and refreshing interchange. They are informed clearly about boundaries of appropriate discussions and always have access to an adult counselor or teacher for debriefing.

Remember: Peer counselors or peer educators need training and supervision in their efforts. Teen helpers or volunteers can easily become personally involved with other teens' problems and can feel overwhelmed. But they can be highly effective with supervision and support.

---

1. Natural Helpers Program. Seattle, WA: Comprehensive Health Education Foundation.

ACTIVITIES IN DYADS

FORMING DYADS/PARTNERSHIPS

Write names of rock groups on strips and cut into two (e.g., Hooty and / The Blowfish, A Tribe / Called Quest). Each person must find his or her "other half." They become partners.

Have each group member find a partner who matches him or her by:
- Having same color of eyes
- Wearing same color shirt
- Being born in same month
- Being born in same state

TRUST WALK

Form pairs. Designate one partner as the Apple and the other as the Orange. Apple will close his or her eyes while Orange leads Apple around the area. They are not to talk. Remind the teens to be careful so others do not get hurt. Tell Apple to stand in front of Orange and fall back.

Discuss with Apples what it feels like to trust the other person:
- What can you do if the person is pushing you too fast?
- What kind of risks are you willing to take?
- What if Orange told you to jump off a wall?
Discuss with Oranges:
- What does it feel like to be responsible for Apple?

(continued)

Expand the discussion to trusting in other relationships:

• What happens when one person has more information than the other?

• What happens if a person has been hurt during this activity before.

Emphasize the need for communication and for time to develop trust in a relationship before taking risks.

BROKEN HEARTS

Cut large hearts out of construction paper. Then cut each heart into two parts. Write half of a statement on each part. Members must find their match to complete the statements accurately. This is a good way to review the content you are teaching in a particular session.

Examples: "AIDS is caused / by a virus." "You cannot get AIDS / by hugging or being near someone who has AIDS."

Discuss the symbolism of broken hearts in relationship to AIDS.

MAGIC STICK ACTIVITY

Paint, name, or decorate an ordinary stick or wand to make it into a "magic stick." Use the magic stick as a microphone to interview a famous person in the group. A facilitator may want to demonstrate this activity first or prepare three or four interview questions. For example:

• Tell us about your amazing discovery/talent/

accomplishment.

- When did you first begin to realize your talent or make your discovery?
- How long did you practice or study to accomplish this?
- What advice would you give others about doing . . . ?
- Is there anyone you want to thank? (This is like the Academy Awards.)

Have the teens find a partner and practice in dyads. Then, the facilitator introduces the activity to the whole group: "Today we are visiting some of the most talented and creative people in the world. In just a moment, our field reporters will interview these up-and-coming stars." The facilitator then hands the magic stick to the first interviewer.

This activity stimulates teens' imagination, hopes, and dreams. Ask group members what it would take to accomplish the feat or success described in their interviews.

Concrete Thinking and the Need
For Structure and Success

In Piaget's terms, adolescents are moving from "concrete operations" to more "formal or abstract operations." This change affects the way they learn, process information, and think about the future. Young teens are quite literal in their descriptions and understanding of events. They often do not make the abstract leaps that adults take for granted. For this reason, they respond well to clear, step-by-step directions, visual cues, and hands-on learning.

One group leader fondly recalled her own concreteness at age 12. Her mother had given her explicit directions for cooking macaroni and cheese. The mother explained how to prepare the white sauce and add the noodles, but failed to tell her daughter to cook the noodles. So the family ended up with cheese sauce over uncooked pasta for dinner.

Tips for Group Leaders

At the first group meeting, establish ground rules.

Negotiating group rules in the first session is generally regarded as standard group procedure. The basic rules cover confidentiality, respect for differing opinions, and consequences for certain behaviors. If you have time, you may choose to let the teens develop the list of rules by themselves, but at the start let them know which rules are nonnegotiable, for example, no alcohol and no illegal activity. Preteens often generate very personal rules, like "No talking about someone's weight" or "No 'your mama' jokes." We feel that rules should be kept to a minimum, but you may want to be flexible with preteens.

If you have time limits and do not want to commit an entire session to the development of group rules, you may want to offer a slate of basic rules that have been developed beforehand by other teens. (Sample Group Rules are found at the end of this chapter.) This slate can include requirements for group participation. For example, a school-based group may include a school-attendance requirement. In other words, if a student misses more than two days of the school week for any reason, he or she will not be allowed to attend group. You can also add rules to the slate, such as "No gossiping about other group members outside the group." Explain the rules and then ask group members if they can endorse the slate. Group members should sign a written copy of the group rules, acknowledging that they are familiar with and agree to the conditions of group participation. This contract helps strengthen members' sense of individual and group ownership.

Help teens maintain confidentiality.

Teens often have difficulty maintaining group confidentiality for the same reasons adults do. Teenagers impulsively share information or tell secrets because they want to be liked or feel it gives them power. Sometimes they unconsciously want to get back at or hurt others. So clearly state up front the consequences for breaches of confidentiality and include confidentiality as a group rule. Ask the teens to discuss how they would feel if someone told their "personal business" outside of group. Indicate that the teens should decide collectively what the consequences will be if someone breaches confidentiality. Avoid a definite "kick-out-policy," because sometimes teens will try to get themselves excluded from the group and you will miss the chance to deal head on with their behavior.

Discuss leader confidentiality and its limits.

Let teens know what information you must share with another adult or authority. This might include situations in which:
- The teen is being physically or emotionally hurt by an adult or family member
- The teen is at risk for harming him- or herself or someone else
- The teen admits to illegal activities

In addition, it is legally mandated in most states that suspicion of child physical or sexual abuse must be reported to local child welfare authorities. This mandate is often extremely troubling for leaders of adolescent groups, who may feel they are betraying a teen who has confided in them. Leaders may also have little confidence in the child welfare system to handle the situation effectively. However, professionals should be aware that if abuse continues or if the child later establishes that the group leader was aware of the abuse and did not report it, the professional could be sanctioned. This policy sometimes inhibits teens from telling the group certain secrets. On other occasions, it may be a teen's way of seeking help.

Promise teens that if you are obligated to report information to another adult or authority, you will do your best to inform the teen directly of this decision. Obviously, in certain legal or crisis situations, this may be impossible. With teens who make suicidal threats, we are willing to risk the teen's temporary anger about revealing this information rather than bear the knowledge alone that a teen is considering ending his or her life.

As a group leader, earn respect and, on occasion, demand it.

Group leaders should not tolerate personal physical threats or offensive personal remarks.

In the early stages of a group, brainstorm together about what respect means and acknowledge that each person must earn respect. If a teen has an outburst or is flagrantly offensive to a leader in a group, tell the teen that you have too much respect for yourself, him or her, and the group to let the behavior continue. Ask the person to leave until he or she can regain self-control. After a few minutes, follow up with the person outside the group to explain the conditions of returning to group.

Keep parents informed and address any concerns about their child's participation in the group.

Parents should always give written permission for a teen to participate in group and these forms should be kept on file. The consent form, however, does not legally obligate you to share confidential issues with parents unless you believe the situation is life threatening. Remember that a parent's endorsement of the group experience is likely to enhance the child's commitment to it as well.

Group leaders' interactions with parents are learning opportunities for both sides. You may find ways to help parents understand the developmental issues that affect their child's relationship and communication patterns. Often parents are frustrated by a teen's focus on self and interpret self-absorption as disrespect or lack of concern for the parent's well-being. Help parents to understand that teens are seeking independence and will demonstrate many push–pull behaviors during the next few years.

Always treat parents with respect. Listen to their concerns. Recognize that they may envy your relationship with their teen, but assure them that you are not trying to take a parent's place. Find creative ways to help teens relate to their parents in different and more constructive ways. For instance, plan special events that showcase each teen's achievements. All parents want to be proud of their sons and daughters. Emphasize the positives!

In addition, find out what parents enjoy and plan activities that allow both parents and teens to shine. Sometimes a class in which both teens and parents learn a new skill offers an equitable, nonthreatening way for them to interact. Some examples include making a holiday ornament, picking up litter in a neighborhood, building a model, and quilting. At events we often ask the teens to be the hosts and choose adults to be their helpers. You can also plan specific activities that will help improve teen–adult communication. Start with team challenges such as getting through an obstacle course or a relay race. Then follow up with interpersonal activities in which teens and parents discuss feelings to promote understanding.

Often parents with whom we work struggle with many of their own relationships and sense of self-worth. Help build their self-esteem and competence in the same way you are helping teens. Model ways to set limits. Model constructive ways to handle feelings. Be REAL with parents just as you are with teens.

Some examples of Parent–Teen Activities are listed at the end of this chapter.

Use pictures, models, simulation games, and clear analogies to teach abstract ideas.

Teens learn best when they can see, touch, or experience what you are trying to convey.

When using analogies, avoid abstract, symbolic ideas. Relate your point to something teens can touch or see. Hands-on team-building activities, for example, vividly demonstrate the abstract concept of "teamwork." In teen-pregnancy-prevention activities, computerized babies that cry when left wet, hungry, or unattended definitely bring the parent experience to life.

For more teaching techniques, see the suggested activities lists at the end of this chapter. They include:

- Activities for Goal Setting
- Activities for Reinforcing Concepts and Content
- Activities for Building Cooperation, Communication, and Group Trust
- Activities for Dealing With Loss and Hurt
- Activities for Dealing With Feelings, Self-Worth, and Labels

Young teens need physical activity and skill practice.

Plan structured ways that allow teens to interact, take responsibility, and learn. In a one-hour therapeutic group, we often begin with an icebreaker of no more than five minutes and a check-in period of 10 minutes. We generally plan one structured activity, which we may or may not use. Always make sure you allow time to process experiential activities. Too many activities with too little time spent considering the implications can destroy the flow of a group.

Reading a computer manual is not the same as punching keys on the keyboard. Learning to say no to sex or drugs takes practice. Knowing how to get an after-school job includes knowing how to fill out an application, what references mean, how to dress, what questions to ask, and so forth. Let teens practice skills, including what to say in a challenging situation. Don't just talk about dealing with pressure; let them act out a scenario and say the words. Don't just talk about making a good impression at a job interview; have them dress the part. Recruit adults to interview teens in a mock interview situation and find other ways to teach skills concretely.

In the early stages of a group, young adolescent boys tend to need more tangible and tactile activity, as opposed to talk sessions.

Use puzzles, fill-in-the-blanks, team competition, games, and role plays as springboards for discussion with boys. This gender difference may be due largely to socialization, in that many girls are encouraged to be affiliative, whereas boys learn early to compete. However, the leader should avoid making assumptions. After older boys trust the group and the leaders, they can be very expressive and often more honest than girls.

In groups, plan events with clear beginnings and endings.

This includes clear agendas, times, and structure for a group series. Try organizing year-long group sessions in phases or themes: Series I (12 sessions), Series II (12 sessions); Part I: Feeling Good—Physically, Mentally, Spiritually (8 sessions), Part II: Working Well—Job Searches, Interviews, and Skills (8 sessions); and so forth. Like adults, teens are more likely to participate if they don't think they are committed for life.

When asking teens about emotional issues, structure the ways you ask questions or present material. In this way, leaders will generally get a more enthusiastic response to an activity or exercise.

Let teens make feeling charts, draw pictures, fill in open-ended sentences, or act out events. (See the suggested Activities for Dealing With Feelings, Self-Worth, and Labels for more ideas.) Then plan time to discuss their responses. Note that seventh and eighth graders may have difficulty role playing someone other than themselves and may need a little help.

Asking for specific responses to questions is helpful. Instead of asking, "How do you feel today?" you might say, "On a scale of 1 to 10, with 1 being very depressed and 10 being super happy, where are you?" Instead of the general query "Tell me what happened this week," try asking group members to describe their morning (when they got up, who was there, and so forth). Or "Tell me the funniest/saddest/most interesting thing you saw today."

Never hesitate to ask teens to "tell me a little more" before you answer a question.

Teens often use colloquial expressions such as "she's fast" or "he messed with me." Group leaders should not assume literal meanings here. Also, some teens will give you the answers they think you want to hear. Ask them to tell you what the phrase means to them, before you assume you know what they mean.

Have teens "talk issues back" to you in group. Ask them to tell you what they understood you to say.

One of the best ways to know how group members have interpreted something is to have them tell it back to you: "Now, let's review what we just talked about. Can you tell me two things you remember?" or "Tell me how you'd describe this to your boyfriend or a friend outside this group."

Videotapes can be fine discussion starters, but remember to preview every video before you use it for age appropriateness and cultural relevance.

Videos should not stand alone in group. They are not meant to baby-sit a group of any age. Always stay in the room while showing a video to observe teen responses to it. Allot time to discuss the video and to emphasize its key points. You might ask teens to look for one or two specific things while viewing the video to help focus their attention, for instance, "Look for what gets John in trouble" or "Watch for information about two ways you can get AIDS."

Young teens also tend to pay too much attention to the physical traits of the actors in videotapes and may miss the point of the video altogether. One way to head this off is to point out humorously before playing the video that a lot of teens have already told you that John's hair is weird or that Ted's lips are too big for his face. Or say that you know the outfits are a little out-dated, but you want them to look past that.

Try organizing a "film-preview panel" of teens to preview and rank films or videos for their effectiveness. Make notes about what they respond to and what they don't seem to understand. This is also a good way to get teens to watch a film without feeling that they are being preached to in a heavy-handed way.

In therapeutic groups, avoid too much insight work with young teens. Instead, create opportunities for them to experience successes and behavioral changes.

It may be helpful for teens to understand the dynamics of loss or abuse or living in an alcoholic family. It can also help them to understand the feelings that lead up to angry outbursts or how people set themselves up for failure and loneliness. However, focusing on the specifics of teens' behavior and helping them to have a different experience in a small group may do them more good than will insight therapy. If adolescents practice a new behavior in a group, with reinforcement and support they can slowly transfer it to the outside world or family.

Sometimes too much insight immobilizes teens or gives them excuses for not moving ahead. Adults can inadvertently reinforce a child's victim status by dwelling on the layers of dysfunction in a family. It is important to offer acceptance and understanding of a child's pain in the group, but also to help teens find concrete ways to make positive strides in their lives.

Young teens can also get stuck because they narrowly or literally interpret what is being said. For example, a teen who has been sexually abused may be overwhelmed by the knowledge that children who have been abused are more likely to abuse others. Children who live in alcoholic families may feel guilty or upset when they learn that there are roles family members often play (the clown, high achiever, and so forth). Often teens understand such roles very literally and may not see their positive aspects.

When leading a short-term group, be very careful not to play psychotherapist and unearth a lot of deep feelings that cannot be dealt with in the time allotted for group. Certainly a leader cannot anticipate what a teen may bring up in group, but he or she should not "peel back all the layers" unless a therapist can follow up or the leader can arrange more intensive therapeutic support for a teen with significant problems.

Teens may not understand process issues in group because the dynamics are too abstract.

Trained group leaders know that groups have content (what is said) and also a process (how and when things are said and the way group members interact with one another). Generally, it is very helpful for a group leader to assess the dynamics in a group after each session.

Frequently, leaders in adult groups will "process" a group, noting who talked first, who rescued whom, and who allied with whom, and will discuss with the group members their roles and behaviors. Although leaders of adolescent groups should also be aware of group process, sharing this information with young teens is often not developmentally appropriate or as enlightening to an adolescent as it may be for adults. Young teens have a little capacity to understand inferences or the more abstract motivations for their behaviors and may be lost in such a discussion.

However, the leader may want to process or discuss an individual group member's explicit self-defeating behaviors in a group. For example, you might note that every time the group brings up a sensitive topic, Joe cracks jokes to take off the pressure. But he gets mad that no one takes him seriously when he is trying to make a point. You might help him to understand how the group gets confused by his behavior. Or the leader can acknowledge that Carla routinely pulls standoffs with school authorities over minor issues every week before group, and these behaviors could jeopardize her being a member of your group. Or every time Susan feels that people are ganging up on her in group, she bursts out of the room.

This kind of processing teaches teens to identify tangible behaviors that they can change or control. These examples are relatively straightforward—based on an observable behavior—as opposed to a more complex dynamic among several members of the group.

One note about confronting a teen's behavior in group: Young teens' egos can be particularly fragile in front of their peers. They may hear feedback better if you tell them individually and suggest ways they can practice a new behavior in group.

Teens' concreteness makes it hard for them to think in terms of future events or consequences.

Teens often romanticize events and they need structured ways to think ahead. Developmentally, they are also beginning to exhibit greater risk-taking behavior.

Teens often cannot imagine that bad things happen to good people. Additionally, they feel an enormous need to act as if they are in total control of most situations in order to compensate for their lack of confidence. Thus, when 14-year-old Tonya tells the group she plans to marry 17-year-old Bobby, her unemployed boyfriend, she truly believes they can live on $150 a month from her baby-sitting job. Some teens also have limited life experiences so they can't even imagine some of the scenarios that jaded adults know so well. Preaching to teens is often a waste of breath; they naturally get defensive.

So don't preach. Instead, tell them you know this will probably never happen to them, but you think it is smart to be prepared. Encourage them to role play how they would handle difficult situations; from baby-sitting crises to riding with an intoxicated friend, from handling a physically abusive date to avoiding a killer fight. Group members can give each other great one-liners and ideas for innovative ways to handle problem situations.

With individual teens, try "what if" scenarios. You might suggest unhappy endings and ask group members to supply alternatives to the negative outcomes.

- What if your boyfriend says, "Prove you love me"?
- What if John challenges you to a fight after school?
- What if you are given a fake ID card to buy alcohol at a convenience store?

Teens can also create a soap opera story out of most any situation. Let one subgroup create romantic endings to the scenario, and let another group create "tear jerker" endings. Watching TV has prepared them royally for this activity.

Repetition is essential.

Teens repeat lots of activities. They comb their hair 44 times a day; they talk on the telephone for hours; they listen to the same CD at every party. So take a tip from them (and TV advertisers). Repeat your messages too—in lively formats, in concrete and experiential forms, with a great big dose of sincerity.

Probably the biggest compliments one group leader we know ever received was from a 15-year-old girl who said that when she went to bed at night, she saw the leader's face and heard the leader's voice encouraging her to stay in school. Teens can listen and learn from you—if you repeat the messages with love, humor, and understanding. Although teens ultimately make their own choices, they make better choices when adults offer them shoulders to cry on and to lean on.

SAMPLE GROUP RULES

1. NO PUT-DOWNS.

Everyone has the right to an opinion, feeling, comment, or question. All points are worthy of being discussed.

2. NO QUESTION IS "DUMB."

Asking questions only says that you want more knowledge or information. Questions do not "tell" anything about the person asking them.

3. TALK ONLY WHEN SOMEONE ELSE ISN'T SPEAKING.

Listening skills are important and indicate respect for others.

4. EVERYONE HAS THE RIGHT TO PASS ON ACTIVITIES OR ON QUESTIONS HE OR SHE DOES NOT WISH TO ANSWER.

There may be times when you do not want to participate in a discussion or activity. But please try to offer something whenever you can.

5. CORRECT TERMINOLOGY SHOULD BE USED WHENEVER POSSIBLE.

If you know the correct term for something, use it. If you don't, use the term you know.

6. EVERYTHING SAID IN GROUP REMAINS IN GROUP.

Confidentiality is important in building trust. Help us to maintain confidentiality by not repeating our discussions outside of the group.

SUGGESTED PARENT-TEEN ACTIVITIES

- Awards banquets or receptions for parents
- Makeovers (mother–daughter makeovers at a local cosmetic counter)
- Fashion shows
- Karaoke songfests
- Needlework and quilting groups
- Road races
- Bicycle trips or relays
- Horseback riding
- Fishing expeditions
- Picnics and swim outings
- Teen dances(for which a parent is the teen's admission ticket)
- Ropes courses or outdoor challenge events
- Hiking trips
- Father's Day and Mother's Day celebrations

ACTIVITIES FOR GOAL SETTING

SHORT-TERM GOALS

Each group member writes down on an index card a goal for him- or herself during the session. Then he or she sits on the card. At the end of the session, members read their cards to determine if they have met their goals.

LONG-TERM GOALS

At the first meeting of the group, ask each teen to write down a goal for the six-week period (or whatever length of time is specified for the group). Hand out postcards to be self-addressed or stationery with envelopes (for privacy). The leader mails these goal statements to the teens at end of the six-week period with encouraging messages. At the three-week mark, the leader may want to remind the teens to recall their goals and assess their progress.

CARS and RELATIONSHIPS

This activity works best with boys, especially our participants in rural areas. We offer it with some reservations. We do not believe women are akin to cars, but the analogy often engages boys in our groups.

Supplies: A cool model car of any size. The facilitator can hold the car or place it on a table in front of the group. The car is a visual enhancement to the discussion.

(continued)

To begin, the facilitator asks the group, "What two things do a lot of guys want when they become teenagers?" Usually, the boys respond with "to drive or own a car" or something about girls.

Ask the group to brainstorm answers to the following questions:

- Do cars and relationships have anything in common?
- What does a car need to work well?
- If you don't take care of a car, what can happen?
- If you ignore noises, what can happen?
- Do we love our cars when they are running well and less so when they are having problems?
- Is a flashy car always a good car?
- What other qualities do you want in a car?

Point out that sometimes the journey in relationships can be bumpy, rough, and full of detours. Cars need care. So do relationships.

ACTIVITIES FOR REINFORCING CONCEPTS AND CONTENT

PIC-CHARADE

Divide the group into teams. Use content words or concepts that the group has learned as the idea to be pictured by means of a drawing or charade. One member of each team must illustrate the concept without talking. When a team guesses the idea or word correctly, its members must make two accurate statements about that word.

THE PRICE IS RIGHT

This game helps teach about the consequences to actions. Set up items and have teens guess the cost. For example, have teams estimate the cost of items involved with parenthood, such as the cost of a hospital delivery, diapers for a month, infant food and clothing, and so forth. The team coming closest to the actual costs without going over gets the point.

BINGO

Put answers to questions about a session's topic in boxes on a bingo card. Use this activity to review content. Ask a question and have students find the answer on their bingo card.

ACTIVITIES FOR BUILDING COOPERATION, COMMUNICATION, AND GROUP TRUST

HEADBANDS

As group members arrive, put an adhesive mailing label on their foreheads with one of the following instructions:

- Be nice to me.
- Don't make eye contact with me.
- Cut me down.
- Act mad at me.
- Ignore me.

Don't let the members see their own instruction as you apply it to their forehead. Then ask the group members to interact with one another, following the instructions on one another's foreheads. After three or four minutes, reconvene the group and ask each person to guess what was on his or her forehead and tell why he or she guessed it. Discuss the ways that members felt when they were ignored or cut down. Discuss how verbal and nonverbal clues show emotions. Use these examples to introduce the idea of nonverbal/verbal communication. Use the activity to reinforce how others' behaviors in group affect our feelings.

GROUP CHAIR

Have the group members stand in a tight circle, all facing sideways in the same direction. They must get close enough to sit on one another's laps. At a signal, everyone sits down on the knees of the person behind him or her.

PAPER PLATE GLOBE

Give out individual paper plates. Ask the teens to draw messages from the group or descriptions of themselves on one or more plates. Staple all the plates together to form a globe, symbolizing how individuals make up a bigger group. Staple each plate on three sides, like a triangle, to ensure that the globe hangs. It takes 20 plates to make a globe.

ACTIVITIES FOR DEALING WITH LOSS AND HURT

GOOD TOUCH/HURTING TOUCH

Brainstorm a list of good touches and harmful touches that group members have experienced. Determine whether you want to keep this activity present oriented, including only touches received within the past year, or reflective, describing touches received as children. Then ask the group to brainstorm how it felt when members received hurting touches. Is it different when someone you love hurts you? The discussion can be expanded to discuss nonviolent ways to handle anger and how we learn to handle anger. You can also explore ways to communicate to another person if he or she is invading your space, pushing unwanted physical intimacy, and so forth.

TORN-UP TEEN

Have teens draw a person at least eight inches in size and cut it out. Now instruct them to pretend that this figure is someone in their family that they "cut down." For every time they have insulted or hurt these people in the last month, tear a piece off the paper figures. (Teens will usually tear enthusiastically.) Then ask them to tape or glue the figure back together.

Discuss this activity. Note that the person never really looks the same after being cut down. You can tape the torn parts, but the scars are still there.

If the same place has been torn over and over, it may not be repairable. The torn places also remain very vulnerable to further stress.

A variation on this activity is to tell the group: "Pretend the drawing is you. Think of someone who has hurt you. Tear off a piece for every time the person has hurt you in the past year. After tearing, try to tape yourself back together." Then discuss the activity and its meaning.

Even with the first variation, teens will often begin relating to the "torn-up person" and may recall people who have hurt them by cutting them down. Be prepared for a lot of self-disclosure on this activity.

THE HEAVY LOAD

This activity helps participants understand how a heavy emotional load can bog them down, stifle communication, and cause them to react differently to others than they might otherwise. This activity also can be helpful in teacher training to raise teachers' awareness of the pressures on at-risk students.

Supplies: A few bricks and a backpack.

Ask one of the participants to put on the backpack. This person will be the one to receive the bricks.

Tell the following story (or make up your own): "Imagine that a student comes to school with a couple of bricks already in his backpack, because one of his parents was drunk last night and on a rampage. The student didn't finish his homework,

(continued)

went to bed late, overslept, and missed the bus. His mother was furious because she had to take him to school, which made her late to work." (Add two bricks to the backpack.)

"When the student gets to school, the teacher confronts him about not having his homework. He doesn't think he can tell her the real reason, so he says, 'I just didn't get around to it.' She tells him his attitude is going to get him into big trouble." (Give another brick.)

"He gets upset, runs out of the classroom, and knocks books out of another student's arms. The other student screams at the boy for being a stupid idiot." (Add another brick.)

"Each time a brick is added, the load gets heavier—and the teen is more off-balance."

Explore these questions with participants:

- What could lighten the load?
- Was the student responsible for any of those bricks?
- What could he have done differently?
- What can friends do if they know a person is carrying a heavy load?
- Ask the students to make up their own scenarios and add bricks to the wearer's pack.

ACTIVITIES FOR DEALING WITH FEELINGS, SELF-WORTH, AND LABELS

A TALE OF TRUE FEELINGS

Cut out magazine pictures of people expressing different emotions. Put these pictures in a paper bag. Have each student choose one from the bag. Ask students to tell the group what they think the person is feeling and to make up a situation in which someone might feel that way. This activity can be adapted by asking the teens to tell the next thing that would be likely to happen to the person pictured.

PAPER BAG DISCLOSURE

Instruct the group members to write words or paste pictures on the outside of a paper bag that describe how others see them. On the inside of the bag, have them write on slips of paper how they see themselves.

Ask questions such as:

• What happens if the "real you" slips out? What would others think?

• Is the inside bag different from the outside bag?

• What does it feel like to keep that a secret?

As participants' trust builds, ask each person to risk telling one thing about the "real me" from inside the bag.

FEELING CHARADES

Write different feelings on cards (hungry, lonely, depressed, violent, and so forth). Hand a card to

(continued)

each student and ask him or her to act out the word without talking while the group tries to guess the feeling being expressed. Can some behaviors, gestures, or expressions be misinterpreted? Stress the importance of checking out what you see before jumping to conclusions.

HOT AIR BALLOON

Instruct group members to pretend they are taking off in a hot air balloon, but several weights are holding them down. Have them label those weights that keep them from taking off and reaching their goals.

FILL IN THE BLANKS

As springboards for discussion, ask students to fill in the blanks on statements such as:
- When I feel sad (or bored/hurt/angry at friends/ angry at my mom or dad), I _____.
- My parents (or teachers) describe me as _____ .
- Girls (or boys) describe me as _____ .

PERCEPTIONS

Supplies: A large picture from a magazine or newspaper.

Cover half of the picture. Ask the group members to give their ideas about what they see or what they think is happening in the picture. Write down all the things they say.

Then remove the cover and show the entire picture. Ask participants if they see it differently now.

Note that many times when we look at a situation, we don't see the whole picture. Remind teens that people have to be careful not to assume or jump to conclusions until they have the whole picture and all the facts.

ARE WE GETTING MIXED MESSAGES?

This activity is a variation on the children's game "Simon Says." The facilitator stands in front of the group and instructs the teens to touch parts of their faces and bodies, as in "Touch the top of your head. Touch your nose. Touch your mouth. Touch your ear." The facilitator should also model the same behavior by touching his or her head, nose, mouth. For the last instruction, say "Touch your nose," but instead touch your chin or the top of your head. Most teens will follow what you do rather than what you say.

Point out that many times actions speak louder than words. Many people will model what they see and not what they hear.

Ask the teens to give examples of how adults may say one thing, but do another. Then ask for examples of how small children will act out what teens do. Stress how important it is to "walk the talk."

The Need for Independence and Exploration of Adult Roles

In one way, young teens are like toddlers. They benefit from structure and supervision as they gain independence. They gain independence in increments, through step-by-step opportunities with adult backup for reinforcement if needed. Unfortunately, many at-risk teens have been emotionally and socially independent since they were small children. Consequently, many have not internalized the skills they need to succeed independently. Group leaders may find that they become surrogate parents of sorts, providing structure and boundaries. Leaders may also find that some 14- or 15-year-olds have the emotional needs of toddlers. You need a big heart and a lot of patience for this job.

Most teen groups want and need some autonomy, but they may need a road map to get there. If group leaders are too controlling, authoritative, or condescending, teen groups will inevitably protest or shut down. On the other hand, most teen groups in the long term respond to guidance from adults and respect adults who set limits.

In our experience, young teens need guidance in establishing topics and agendas for group. If the group leader is totally nondirective, the lack of structure often causes the group to flounder, which can frustrate members, the facilitator, and the group's sponsoring organization. It is also very difficult to evaluate a group's effectiveness if it has no explicit goals.

The need for guidance from the leader does not override the need to assess teens' most pressing concerns. Early on, the facilitator can solicit group input through verbal or written activities. In a sexuality-issues group, for example, the leader asked the girls to write down the three questions they always wanted to know about relationships and sexuality. Their responses ranged from "What is an erection?" to "Why does my mom let her boyfriend hit her?" The group facilitator then incorporated these concerns into upcoming curriculum.

Often group leaders plan to offer a series of speakers to teens for variety and different expertise. Remember, though, that teens need a consistent adult as well to tie together themes and to offer an ongoing relationship. Too many shifts in speakers and styles can limit the development of trust and growth in a group.

As a group leader, you present a behavior style that may be similar to or different from that of other significant adults in the teens' lives. Leaders model values and behavior in the ways they nurture and affirm teens, show affection to them, display frustration and anger in group, negotiate conflicts, and in what leaders think is humorous.

Many teens in therapeutic groups have witnessed inappropriate adult behaviors at home. Because of this, they may expect rejection, lack of emotional support, confusion, and loss in their relationships with adults. Teens are especially needy and vulnerable in their interactions with group leaders.

Tips for Group Leaders

Use structure more than authority to shape group behaviors.

Structure often makes teens feel more secure initially—even though they may gripe about it. For example, one group leader found that if teens ate refreshments all through group, there were often many interruptions. You might consider serving refreshments only at the end of the group.

Leaders also can shape behaviors without saying a word. For example, in an after-school program, only teens who arrived on time could register for a door prize.

It is easier to relax structure in groups as the participants demonstrate their ability to monitor themselves than to create structure after the group has gone bananas. For example, before an outside speaker addresses your group, review appropriate group behavior with members and determine consequences if someone doesn't comply. In addition, you may want to set ground rules for use of a group room or other property that will be utilized by the group.

Setting standards ahead of time allows you to be less authoritarian and also gives you the chance to commend groups for being responsible, attentive, mature, polite, and so forth.

Assign responsibilities to teens in the group.

As leader, avoid assuming all the responsibility for special events. Let teens discover the work involved in undertaking projects such as field trips and community service efforts. Let teens help monitor other teens while on bus trips or outings.

Teens in groups need ways to achieve. In school-based groups, one teen may handle the sign-in chart and another can give out the door prizes. In a teen moms' group, two teens were assigned to manage the group store where teens traded special stamps for baby supplies. In after-school groups, teens have planned and executed special events ranging from fashion shows and craft booths to entrepreneurial businesses.

Avoid micromanaging groups, but assert yourself when it is necessary to do so.

Your tone of voice makes a difference here. Teens will often put on makeup, comb their hair, doodle, walk around, or have individual conversations in groups. Sometimes a look or hand on the shoulder will stop the behavior, but don't assume the teen will get the message. If you feel a behavior is distracting, you should specifically ask the offender to stop. You may need to use an "I statement" ("I would like you to put away your makeup, because I want to see your face!" or "I can't hear John if you guys keep talking").

One person's behavior may not be distracting by itself, but a behavior multiplied times 10 or 20 has different repercussions. Once we asked 14 eighth-grade girls in group to get out their combs and brushes. We all combed our hair while trying to carry on a group discussion. Obviously, we were doing this humorously—but the girls got the point.

If group members challenge you, listen to their arguments. Then determine whether the issue is negotiable.

It may be helpful to problem solve situations with group members, if you feel that group behavior is inappropriate or offensive. But at times the entire group may not find the behavior offensive or may feel too intimidated to say so. Therefore you, as group leader, may have to assert that the behavior is not acceptable to you in the current environment.

Once, during a coed teen group, a girl put her head in her boyfriend's lap while group members were talking. The girl began rubbing her boyfriend's leg. The leader found this behavior totally distracting. She realized that the group members had become accustomed to it and would not risk angering the girl. So the leader told her that she wanted the girl to sit up to help the leader concentrate. The teen was huffy, but complied. Later, the leader and the young woman talked about her behavior. The young woman still did not think it was a big deal but agreed to comply with the leader's wishes to improve the leader's concentration.

Some teens will run all over you if you have no obvious boundaries. The leader should set clear limits related to destruction of property, weapons, unruly behavior, and so forth. Sometimes it helps to enlist the most ardent "resisters" as group bouncers or as your assistants in planning, although they may need close supervision to stay on task.

Establish a teen council or review committee to solve problems that may arise in group.

SORRY TOM, NO WEAPONS

Teen councils can provide helpful ideas and strategies to help larger groups work more effectively, although leaders should be forewarned that sometimes peers can be quite punitive in determining consequences for unacceptable group behaviors. Members still need adult guidance in making these decisions.

Teens can gain self-esteem and learn responsibility through community service projects, but don't forget to continue nurturing the teen group while it is giving to others.

One of the most enlightening experiences we ever had in directing a teen community service project was with a group of seventh-grade girls who were assigned as "big sisters" to a group of low-functioning first graders at a local elementary school. The seventh graders were thrilled at this opportunity to be "big sisters" and had a heightened sense of their importance. Interestingly, however, they were very competitive with the younger children. Instead of encouraging the first graders to play with the toys we had brought, the seventh graders vied for the toys themselves. When they made friendship bracelets for the first graders, we needed to make friendship bracelets for every older girl in the group too. And the seventh graders wanted to make sure that they always got treats and refreshments if their "little sisters" were getting some.

Clearly, this experience taught us that teens who have unmet physical and emotional needs cannot give from an empty vessel. In this case, the older girls needed the same level of attention as the younger children, and then some.

If teens plan to undertake a community or charity project to serve another group of teens who may have fewer resources or more stressful life situations than do the group members, leaders should remember that children who are receiving help often already feel very vulnerable. Having another teen deliver the help can be even more disheartening. If teens are involved in such projects, ensure that the activities involve all the teens equitably (e.g., building a Habitat for Humanity house, cleaning up a neighborhood) so that all of the teens benefit from the exchange.

Teens are naturally curious about your personal life and may ask you very blunt questions.

You have the right—and sometimes the responsibility—not to answer every personal question teens ask you. These may include questions about your sexual history, your marital relationship, your children, your substance or alcohol use.

Sometimes the teenagers are really seeking your advice about their own issues. Other times they are just downright curious. You can respond in a respectful tone: "Sounds like you're really interested in my family—but let's talk about you right now." You can also humorously say: "That's my business—just like some things are your business." Your tone is very important in these exchanges. You want to convey "openness" but maintain boundaries. We are very cautious about personal self-disclosures that can be misconstrued or used out of context. We have witnessed reprisals by parents or community advocates against group leaders who have acknowledged early sexual experimentation or alcohol use.

> *Young teens may experience emotional conflict as they observe healthy adult behaviors that challenge or contradict their previous experiences with parents or other adults in their lives.*

Often children may act surprised if the leader does not fit a stereotype having to do with gender or roles. For example, several boys may be shocked that in the leader's family boys do dishes or that parents do not physically punish children.

Teens may idealize the group leader and reject their parents. They may also use what the group leader says or does as ammunition against their parents.

Responsible group leaders should listen empathically to teens' woes concerning their parents and not automatically switch into a defense of the parents. Eventually, however, leaders should assist the teens in improving communication with their parents or in addressing the realities of their parents' lives. The group leader should not compete with the parent for attention or tear down the parent even further.

Young teens are prone to hero worship and can be dev-
astated emotionally by disappointment in their hero's
behavior, ethical errors, and other imperfections.

It is often helpful to discuss how teens have felt
when they were shocked or hurt by a hero's behavior
(such as drug use, illegal activity or reckless behaviors).
If the hero or heroine happens to be the group leader,
members need the space and emotional support from
other adults to be angry, express disappointment, and
process their emotions.

Young teens often have romantic fantasies about
or crushes on group leaders and other adults they
admire. They may seek attention from the leader
indirectly or in overt ways.

If the leader feels that these dynamics are interfering
with the interaction in the group, he or she should:

• Meet with the teen individually after group (in a
room with an open door). Inform your coleader about
the meeting. You may want your coleader to be present
during the discussion.

• Acknowledge the teen's feelings. Do not minimize his
or her emotions.

• Do not reject the teen but be clear with him or her
about the limits of your relationship.

• Do not give mixed messages. State your message
clearly: "I think you are feeling a closeness with me
because of X. I care about you and I am here to help
you in dealing with X. But I want to be clear that I have
no romantic feelings for you." Clarify any behaviors
that you feel may be confusing: "When I hug you or pat

you on the back, I care about you but I am not expressing romantic feelings for you." If the leader feels
uncomfortable by any physical expression displayed by
the teen, he or she may also comment on this and suggest ways to modify the behavior.

> Adolescent group members will often project posi-
> tive and negative feelings on you and your coleader
> and may try to split you off from each other, much
> as they might try to manipulate parents. Avoid
> becoming allied with the teens against your
> coleader. Keep communication lines open between
> the two of you.

Group coleaders should always be aware of the
roles they assume in group—and of the need for balance. For example, if one coleader always ends up
being the heavy and the other more fun, the leaders
may need to balance their roles. Coleaders obviously
cannot and should not be carbon copies of each other,
but they should continually assess ways in which their
roles complement and conflict.

In interacting with group leaders, teens often play
out their experiences at home. With male and female
coleaders, group members may assume that the male
coleader is the authority figure or imagine a romantic
relationship between the coleaders. In this case, coleaders have a great opportunity to model a platonic, coop-
erative relationship, which might well represent to the
teens an unfamiliar way of relating between the sexes.

Teens can also sense if tensions or unresolved issues
exist between group coleaders. Remember that the teens
should not be your sounding board for disagreements. If

you have concerns about or conflicting styles with your coleader, discuss these issues between yourselves.

If teens tell you they don't like your coleader or they think she is too nosy, he doesn't listen, and so forth, listen to the teens but also encourage them to tell the coleader directly about their concerns. You may also want to discuss these issues with your coleader, particularly if you have observed that his or her behaviors have indeed built barriers with the group.

It is usually helpful (though a little scary) for coleaders to give each other feedback about leadership styles, group issues that have personal impact, and kids that seem to "push your buttons." Coleading a group is a marriage of sorts—each partner has strengths and blind spots—and yet together you both may make a great team. Just remember that teamwork takes practice, too.

Adolescent group work often evokes the leaders'
own emotional issues, adolescent memories, and life
experiences.

Teen groups often deal with issues of sexuality, loss, grief, relationships, self-image, and risk taking. It is essential that group leaders be clear about their own emotional and sexual needs to ensure that they do not make inappropriate demands of the group. This is not to say that group leaders should leave their humanity aside, but adults have other means through which to meet their own emotional needs. Always acknowledge expressions of caring from the group, but assure the members that you are finding help, relaxation, and resolution to your own problems from other sources.

Conclusion

Remember when we compared leading groups to learning to drive a car? We hope this manual has given you a little driver's education and a few tips on how to stay on the road. In particular, keep your radar tuned for the developmental needs of teens: the need for attention, acceptance, action, and authoritative guidance. Try a few of our road tips and see if they work in your groups. Through activities, steer teens to better communication and understanding of themselves and others. Create welcome stations, road signs, amusements, and successes along the way. Include parents on the journey whenever you can. If your group starts to sputter, check the fuel gauge and ask the teens to analyze the problem. Let the teens help steer the group, too; they learn to drive by watching and imitating you.

The road trip can take many routes. This book suggests ways to structure activities and handle the unexpected, but undoubtedly you will discover new paths along the way. Getting to your destination is only part of group activity; understanding the process and the sights along the way can be just as important. Leaders will want to make the road trip full of fun, food, and friendship. Those memories last a lot longer than recollections of the curricula you used.

Remember, too, that changing road conditions are part of the journey. Stay flexible and forgiving. Allow yourself to learn from teens, and they will certainly learn from you. Be REAL and give teens permission to do the same. Finally, we encourage you to keep the driver in tip-top condition. Neither groups nor drivers can run on empty. So treat yourself and your group and fill up on premium once in a while, with our compliments!

So take good care of yourself and take advantage of the opportunities for personal and professional growth provided by working with groups of adolescents. We hope that this guidebook will contribute to your enjoyment of the ongoing journey and wish you continued success in the important contributions you are making in the lives of young people.

Additional Resources for Group Work and Work With Adolescents

Benson, Jarlath F. Working More Creatively With Groups. London: Routledge, 1993.

Corder, Billie F. Structured Adolescent Psychotherapy Groups. Sarasota, FL: Professional Resource Press, 1994.

Corey, Gerald. Theory and Practice of Counseling and Psychotherapy, 5th ed. Pacific Grove, CA: Brooks/Cole, 1996.

Corey, Gerald. Student Handbook for Theory and Practice of Counseling and Psychotherapy. Pacific Grove, CA: Brooks/Cole, 1996.

Corey, Marianne Schneider, and Corey, Gerald. Groups, Process and Practice, 4th ed. Pacific Grove, CA: Brooks/Cole, 1992.

Dossick, Jane, and Shea, Eugene. Creative Therapy I: 52 Exercises for Groups and Creative Therapy II. Sarasota, FL: Professional Resource Exchange, 1988, 1991.

Dumont, Larry. Surviving Adolescence: Helping Your Child Through the Struggle to Adulthood. New York: Villard, 1991.

Fleming, Martin. 101 Support Group Activities—For Students Affected by Chemical Dependence. Minneapolis, MN: Johnson Institute.

Jacobs, Edward. Group Counseling: Strategies and Skills. Pacific Grove, CA: Brooks/Cole, 1988.

For General Inspiration in Work With Teens

Carrera, Michael. Lessons for Lifeguards. New York: Donkey Press, 1996.

Good, E. Perry. Helping Kids Help Themselves. Chapel Hill, NC: New View Publications, 1990.

Natural Helpers Program. Seattle, WA: Comprehensive Health Education Foundation.

Piaget, Jean. The Origins of Intelligence in Children. New York: International Universities Press, 1952.

Wiltens, Jim. No More Nagging, Nitpicking, and Nudging. Sunnyvale, CA: Deer Crossing Press, 1991.